Following The

Hoofprints

Following The Hoofprints

From unteachable child

to student horse whisperer

By Charlie Avent

Foreword by Monty Roberts

This book has been designed and published in collaboration with The Autism Directory Publishing and CreateSpace

ISBN 978-1497437067

CONTENTS

FOREWORD

In mid 2012 I had a conversation with Kelly Marks my first certified instructor. She informed me that she had completed a course that included a very interesting student. Kelly told me that his name was Charlie Avent and that he was 24 years of age. I was then informed that Charlie was born with what he describes as a special gift called 'Autism'.

Kelly went on to discuss with me the possibility of including Charlie in one of my evening demonstration events taking place at Hartpury College, Gloucester on the 2nd November 2012. It is well established that I work as much with people as I do with horses and the suggestion intrigued me. The challenge was to put together an experience that the young man could handle.

It was mid-afternoon when I was introduced to Charlie and we were scheduled to include his segment at about 9.30 that evening. Charlie amazed me with what appeared to be an extreme zest for life and a profound interest in horses that he claimed gave him a reason to live. Immediately it was clear that Charlie exhibited repetitive movement syndrome.

When excited about something Charlie would smile or laugh like anybody else but his unique characteristic was to slap himself all over. Slapping his legs and his chest, his arms would fly like a wild drummer. His actions were evidence of his gleeful recognition of what horses had meant to him in dealing with his gift. Charlie was a happy young man and obviously pleased to be with us.

We conducted a short trial session with one of Kelly's horses just so that I could be certain that Charlie would be safe and could demonstrate to the audience that he was capable of achieving what we call 'Join Up'. Charlie passed his rehearsal test with flying colours and seemed to be more at home while working with the horse than he was outside talking with us.

The time came, we had been on a 30 minute interval and I met with Charlie and walked toward the centre of the ring talking with him about what we were going to demonstrate for the audience of 1100 people. It was then that I was thrown my first significant curve with our idea regarding Charlie Avent. He said 'I can do the horse but I don't think I can talk in front of an audience that big'.

Charlie told me that he had never spoken to such a large group of people and he just didn't believe that he would feel comfortable. I told Charlie not to worry for a minute. 'If necessary' I said 'I will do all the talking and you can just work with the horse'. I told him that if he chose to speak he could just visit with me and forget that there was an audience there at all.

As we approached the round enclosure in the centre of the arena I pointed out that they had placed two chairs facing the audience, right in the middle. I told Charlie that he would be holding a microphone but he would only need it if he chose to speak with me. We entered the round pen and the audience was quite respectful as I introduced Charlie.

Explaining Charlie's challenge as tactfully as I could I was concerned about the factor of embarrassment. I carefully asked Charlie first one question and then another. His words came, a little haltingly, at first and then he began to converse with me in a quite normal fashion. I remember sitting there feeling extreme admiration of this young man as he spoke.

It seems to me that it was about four or five questions into our conversation that Charlie was describing what horses meant to him. The next thing I know, he is up out of his chair and walking up and down in front of the audience having an in depth conversation about how horses, the Kelly Marks' course he took, and my inviting him to be there affected his life.

It seems to me that for four or five minutes Charlie wowed the audience with a grasp of understanding that none of us knew existed. I had to get up, go to him and literally thank him and take his mike away in order to get down to the business of working with the horse. Charlie Avent is a student that has reached a memorable status seldom achieved in my career.

It seems to me that it was on that night that Charlie informed me he wanted to write a book and hoped that it would help other people gifted with autism. He asked me if I would do the foreword for his book. I explained that I would consider it an honour and that it was one of the most gratifying requests I have ever received. It pleases me to complete our agreement.

Anyone born with autism that has the ability to read will be blessed by the words in this book. Those who cannot execute reading but can be read to, will likewise benefit greatly. Now, for those who consider themselves 'normal' let me suggest to you that there is an enormous amount that can be learned from the words of Charlie Avent. It pleases me to present his book to you.

Monty Roberts

DEDICATIONS

This book is dedicated to all those with disabilities or learning difficulties in recognition of their inspirational courage, to all the horses who have taught me, and all the humans who supported me.

Charlie Avent

INTRODUCTION

My name is Charlie Avent. Although I live a normal life in the United Kingdom, I have a special gift called Autism which means I'm very sensitive to the world around me. This is my true story of how a horse named Oscar saved my life and helped me to become a Horse Whisperer.

This helped me to turn my Autism into a gift that I now use to help me communicate with horses and other Autistic people as well as teaching neuro-typical people to be more autism friendly.

There are many adventures I have had as a direct result of my Autism and many of them were amazing. I do hope you enjoy reading about all my many adventures and experiences.

A CHEQUERED START

I was born in December 1987 as a normal-looking child with a loving and devoted mother and father. However there were difficulties from the start which worried my parents who struggled to understand me.

My younger brother Laurence was born when I was 19 months old. Laurence was always the sporty and athletic one. He was clever at school and later he studied maritime law at university. Laurence and I were two opposite people as my interests were centred around Star Wars at the time I was at school, but Laurence loved football and sport. Despite our different strengths and interests, Laurence and I had plenty of fun building dens in the woods and even making a tree house many years later in a huge beech tree with help from our father.

We struggled for many years on a low income and this took its toll on my parents.

From the start of my life I knew I was different from those around me. I couldn't quite work it out and this drove me crazy. The knowing I was utterly different but not knowing why or how was one of the hardest challenges I faced. Primary school was hard, and because of my difficulties I went to 3 different primary schools. Only Callington Primary School really ever worked for me as I had a really kind teaching assistant who helped me. I joined in with the netball team as I was on friendly terms with several girls.

I have always found girls less threatening and easier to get along with, mainly perhaps because many of the males in my life felt threatened by my Autism and didn't know how to cope with it, and this turned them hostile and even violent towards me.

I think that many of these boys who picked on me were jealous that I was so good at charming the ladies even at 8 years old, and that's probably why I was bullied so badly in school! Although I had an OK time in Callington Primary School, I had an awful time in every school before and after.

FAMILY LIFE MEMORIES

My childhood memories are a strange mixture, as my father and I did some fun things but also some dangerous things together. This included once dismantling a firework display rocket to see what was inside it and work out how it worked. As soon as we opened the firework we found many different coloured powders; reds greens yellows blues and blacks as well as many other colours! Some people might describe this activity as reckless, but from my perspective it was science that meant something and felt real unlike the trashy national curriculum lessons at school that were almost entirely written and theory work based!

My dad also taught me what materials were most flammable and more importantly why petrol was less useful for lighting bonfires and very dangerous compared to diesel, which is slow burning and not explosive so it is safer and burns at a greater temperature. Fire is and has always been a source of fascination for me and I'm often asked to light the fire for people at the stables.

It's fair to say that though my father and I loved each other very much neither of us ever knew quite what to make of the other in those early years as he found my Autism extremely hard to understand and cope with. I suspect my father and his family have Autism traits as they are all intelligent and gifted but quite set in their own interests, such as maths, engineering, archaeology and boats.

Once, we fetched my mum a wonderful Mother's day present in the form of a huge piece of driftwood shaped like the top of a vast mushroom from the beach in the dead of night with a wheelbarrow, and my dad remarked on how the whole thing had looked very suspicious!

My father worked as a cabinet maker in my early years and later he built masts and spars for sailing boats. Unfortunately he struggled to make a living because many people were into plastic boats and metal masts, which made things hard at times.

My mother had a small holding and we kept chickens, ducks, geese, goats and Shetland sheep there. I remember when the sheep had lambs, mum would let me lie in the pen with them at 4 in the morning and cuddle them! At one stage we even had pigs. My mum has always been an amazing cook although that's true of many mums. Because we grew our own organic fruit and vegetables and had fresh meat from either our own animals or the local farmers market, we lived well despite a very tight budget.

Sadly despite both being wonderful people in their own ways my parents decided that they were not right for each other and this led to my father finding a new partner and this led to a divorce. I enjoyed visiting my father at weekends and sometimes we would go sailing and fishing with him on his boat Lundy Lady or we would be making huge bonfires at his new partner's house.

Not long after my parents went their separate ways my mother took my brother and I to the Isle of Skye which I would have loved but I got ill at the beginning of the trip as I often did back in those days. One interesting part of the journey was being given a tour of the Boeing 737's cockpit as the pilots chatted to me about how the plane worked. I can remember the HUD or "Heads Up Displays" being blue with white writing on the screens like in the movies.

I remember the complex computers all displaying information to the flight teams. The radar scope was my favourite gadget as I could see 3 blips from smaller aircraft nearby.

I loved the flying and found it hard to even sit still in my seat but found it much harder when the cabin pressure adjusted in my ears as this caused a huge sensory input overload as well as hurting my ears a lot! When the plane landed we met with mum's friend and her children in The Isle of Skye and they showed us around. They told us about some of the Scottish wildlife like eagles and I was very excited by this; although we never saw any.

MY CHALLENGING LIFE

I was diagnosed in 1997 with Autism, Asperger's Syndrome, A.D.H.D (Attention Deficit Hyperactivity Disorder) and Dyspraxia.

They tried medication like Ritalin and much later a new drug called Strattera to help me control my difficulties but I suffered awful side effects. I will try now to describe these for you as best I can even though it means bringing back a nasty memory.

I felt really tired, drained and limp to begin with, then as they tried increasing the dosage to see if things improved, I started to feel dizzy, sick, shaky, floppy and as if I had no energy to stand let alone do anything.

I became so ill that I had to spend large amounts of time that should have been productive school time lying on the classroom floor feeling so ill that I thought I was going to pass out, then getting nagged to get on with my work which made me feel much worse as no one seemed to care how scared and ill I felt.

I began refusing to take any form of medication and demanded to be taken off the medications they had tried due to the horrid side effects.

I am now a big disbeliever in the use of non-homeopathic medications and to this day cannot understand why my doctor increased the doses of the medication when I felt ill at first instead of totally ending it immediately. I think medication should only ever be used to treat a real medical problem like my epilepsy.

To try to help me, I had a variety of special diets such as 'gluten free', but these made me feel singled out as if punished for being Autistic as the range of food I already ate was extremely limited and I struggled to find anything I liked on the diets at all. I was not impressed with dairy free chocolate or gluten free cakes as they don't taste of much at all in my opinion!

Hoping to find activities I could be involved in, my father and mother decided to take Laurence and I to Beavers and Cubs. This didn't work well for me, and I spent more time on the roof of the Cub hut than inside it, feeling scared of the other people yet excited at having freedom!

I can try to describe the feelings I had about climbing on the roof for you, it felt like fear and anxiety and a feeling of excitement all rolled into one, a need to escape and not be caught or easy for other people to reach as if I felt threatened by them although to this day I can't think why.

At several points my mum sent me to a respite holiday centre run by Vitalize called Church Town Farm for people with disabilities where they have holidays doing boating and climbing as well as swimming. Here, I first was very homesick and was reluctant at first to even try it but really loved it once I met some new friends.

These new friends included pretty female student nurses and student therapists who were working at the centre as volunteer carers to gain experience in the care industry. Many of them came from all over the world and I also enjoyed talking to the foreign visiting support workers hearing about far away countries.

I struggled through mainstream school. I was lonely, angry and felt that few people wanted to listen to me because I was different. This caused me to believe that I should give up on achieving anything. I became extremely hard to motivate and very challenging to cope with, only my family and my wonderful community nurse, Tina Earl, seemed to have any wish to really help.

For most of my school life I was in mainstream education and became increasingly frustrated and angry that my teachers couldn't see my true problems with written tasks and processing instructions or concentration.

Things became much worse as the other students began bullying me, they beat me up and stood on me on the floor, kicked me around the playground and called me all kinds of filthy names that have no place in this book.

Things got even worse, when right in the middle of all this the house I lived in with my mum and brother was burgled. It happened on my mum's birthday, and was totally ransacked. I was so afraid and so angry that I slept with an improvised weapon beside me at night and was barely able to sleep for months afterwards. The problems at school made it worse and in turn my behaviour deteriorated more and more. Eventually the commoners at the comprehensive school I attended at the time decided they didn't want me there any longer and threw me out.

After the burglary, my mum decided that we needed a dog again. Our previous family dog, Meggie, was an old collie cross, and had been unwell and put to sleep a few months prior to the break-in.

Meggie was a lovely dog who looked after my brother and I like a nanny especially in our younger years even letting me lay down with my head on her tummy when I felt upset or ill. Meggie and I loved to lie beside the range.

Meggie's death hit us very hard, especially my mum. We took on a rescued collie called Treacle, and I remember going to the dog home to meet him. He was adorable, but it soon became clear that he was a former abuse case, so consequently he was very fearful and neurotic. He clearly expected the worst of humanity. Shortly after we got him he attacked me thinking I was going to hurt him when I was upset.

I promised mum I would try hard to be calm around Treacle to try to gain his trust, but one terrible, sad day he attacked me in an all-out assault. He had to be dragged off me by mum, still trying to savage my wrists. I was covered in blood and still carry the scars on my arms to this day. It was all I could do to stop him getting near my face as he mauled my wrists and hands let alone calm him or myself down. I was more upset about Treacle being put to sleep later that evening only half an hour from the attack than the fact that he could have seriously injured or even killed me.

I hope God looks after him in heaven because he was clearly a good person who like me had a difficult start.

I will always remember Treacle for the day we swam together in the sea at the Cornish fishing village of Coverack, he was swimming around barking and chasing me in the water!

I was treated like filth right through mainstream school, and far from the teaching staff stopping the abuse, it seemed to me that many of them joined in during lessons by constantly threatening me with detentions and shouting and swearing at me.

One teacher even physically kicked me (I think she knew I was too afraid to tell anyone the truth as I was a scared little child at the time and as no one witnessed it, there was no chance of any help from anyone anyway). At school I would walk out of the school gates or climb onto the roof of the nearest classroom to escape the teachers and bullies and this led to my label of unteachable child.

Break and lunchtimes at school for me consisted of dodging the bullies and teachers and trying to stay away from anyone who looked scary including anyone new or different. I think this might be why I fit with horses and ponies well after all we both have a strong fight or flight response and are both hyper-sensitive to our surroundings.

Sadly for all around me the increased amounts of violence I was facing at school led to me becoming extremely aggressive and nasty to be around at home and this led to me being branded with behavioural problems like many other children. I became almost full of hate to the point that I used to take it all out on my brother and mum often physically attacking and hurting them with pieces of wood or metal.

I began to hate myself for even having Autism and couldn't understand why God would give me such a punishment. As my behaviour got worse and my confidence dropped to rock bottom many of my teachers and even some so called health professionals started to say that I was a hopeless case who needed 24 hour care.

One of only a small number of professionals who continued to believe in me was a lovely and very kind, hard-working community nurse called Tina Earl. She would often come to visit and try to help my family figure out what to do next with her colleague Tom, the educational psychologist.

I was often cuddling and rough with the pets and animals at home and although I my intent was not malicious, I was often over the top with over cuddling the cat or dog. My treatment of animals back then was full on and at times cruel. I saw animals as my comfort from the evil I faced around me.

Sadly, because I was so scared and angry, the animals had a rough time though I loved them very much.

At one stage I had a wonderful cat called Shadow who was my one good friend in those dark days. Shadow was a tiny kitten and when I met him first I fell in love straight away. I hung out hunting with Shadow and watched him hunt and kill a grey squirrel when he was only 1 year old. Sadly he died of an unknown disease not very many months after and I was devastated.

I feel sad about Shadow even now as I write this book.

"Shadow wherever you are now I love you very much, we will see each other again, rest in peace brother".

One very happy memory I have was when my brother went off to Kenya with his school and to prevent me feeling left out Mum took me on holiday to the Isles of Scilly in Cornwall to go fishing and exploring. This is my ideal place as I know each island well and felt safe there even left alone fishing. We went for tea and chocolate cake in a little tea room. I also researched the history of the islands especially the military history. I had a wonderful time exploring the islands.

My mum also took me to Rock Meets Blues in the park, a festival of rock 'n roll at a National Trust house called Lanhydrock House. This was great for me but overloading too. I loved the fireworks at the end and we saw a Queen tribute band.

When I visited my father I sometimes would be able to go sailing with him. Once we went sailing and fishing from Plymouth to Newton Ferrers to cook our catch of mackerel on the camp fire while my dad's dog, a Hungarian Vizsla called Merlin, bounded around the beach, chasing gulls and pretending to be a hippo wallowing in rock pools. I love, and always have loved, fire as it seems to warm my heart when I feel fed up and it looks so bright and cheerful. I like burning rubbish and watching wood glow red then slowly turn to ash.

My mother, who had always liked riding, tried taking my brother and I horse riding at the local riding school. My brother decided that horses were not his thing while I really wanted to learn, but struggled in the traditional riding school environment and found it all but impossible to understand the instructor shouting things like "left rein right leg" or asking me to perform a Half Pass which made me see a picture in my head of half a loaf of bread and a car speeding past it!

My mind pictures things very literally and so I often will take a minute to work out what someone says. In a school situation this led my teachers to think that I was either thick or being deliberately awkward and stubborn. I have found that short clear sets of instructions are nearly always the best thing for me and I recommend teachers adopt this as a basic rule.

When I rode out on hacks, I learned from the horse how to walk, trot and canter and I felt free and happy for a while, but this didn't last long because I still felt that something was missing in my life with equines.

I will admit that the traditional horsemanship methods really upset me. I find it hard to understand how anyone can justify hitting an animal like a horse with a whip whilst calling it their friend, or use forceful gadgets to strap it's head down to its chest, or tie its mouth shut. I gave up on horse riding after several years of lessons deciding that while the humans physically ruled the horses with threats and force and pain it seemed little better than slavery.

From the beginning of my time with the horses I wanted to know more about the way they communicated with each other. I could see real communication between horses but I couldn't understand what was being said. In those days few knew about the only real form of true horsemanship, the horse's body language of Equus, and I certainly didn't have a clue.

My mum looked into respite care and arranged for me to begin going to a carer at their house after school at first, then over some weekends. Sometimes carers came to look after me at home too, which was great in some ways as it gave me some new structure. It wasn't very good when carers were not trained for working with children with autism and learning difficulties, or 'A.S.T' – 'Autism Spectrum Tools' as I now call it, as some were rude, others were full of themselves and the rest were clueless. One man who looked after me was not well trained for Autism and his son often liked to threaten me with air rifles and pistols and knives for a joke. I found it all very frightening as I couldn't tell if the gun was loaded or not, but obviously I'm still alive even though that isn't the point.

Autistic Spectrum 'Disorder' implies something is wrong with me and it made me feel like I was a worthless freak and a mutant to hear people saying I had Autistic Spectrum Disorder, I found it extremely hurtful as anyone would.

Not all of us with Autism express their feelings as clearly as I do but everyone has feelings and I think if more carers could show more emotional intelligence towards their clients it could really help everyone. Clearly something is very right with me if I can speak to horses, play the drums, help others with Autism and do public speaking; not to mention train and ride horses without tack!

I believe that Autism is what you make it, like most things in life, only we have the power to change our perceptions and attitudes and only we have the power to turn our Autism into a constructive tool for good.

AUTISM ADVICE TO PARENTS/CARERS

The trick with Autism is the following: firm boundaries are essential between both a person who has Autism and those around them with **mutual** respect. People around them should be polite, using please and thank you, regardless of whether the person with Autism is verbal, and there should be plenty of warmth, love and affection. Focus on what people **can** do and encourage their interests and these will become strengths. You never know what that odd habit of stacking things in odd places and orders might, one day, grow into.

I never got invited out to friends' houses as a child mainly because the few children who I hung around with were from families who thought I would pass Autism onto their children. Unfortunately I can't cause someone to catch Autism although I believe that if I could give someone Autism they would mentally collapse under the amazing thoughts feelings and sensory overloads I can get at times. I felt like other people saw a mutant when they looked at me and a target to use and abuse.

AUTISM ADVICE FOR SCHOOL CHILDREN

If you are reading this before going to school, try to think if there is someone in your class or school that has a difficulty? Maybe try talking to them the next time you see them; you might end up making friends and maybe you will find lots of cool new things to talk about. Only you have the power to end abuse and bullying in your school and that should be your main concern. Please don't become weak-minded and fearful by bullying. You must make your own choice in the playground about how to deal with bullying. Will you show Spirit and I some true grit like legendary cowboy and horse whisperer Monty Roberts, and find a non-violent way to help those in need?

I still feel anger when I think of the bullying even now as this demonstrates no emotional intelligence at all on the part of those who bully and makes me feel very sad and scared for the future of humanity.

I still don't understand why they were so afraid, but that is a bully for you, they are scared and so they gang up to act tough.

I lost the will to live because I was surrounded by a mob of nasty people in the playground every day and beaten and taunted and insulted for almost 16 years. During the time I was in school being bullied I lost lots of weight and used to feel so anxious about the next school day that I would feel sick and refuse food for days at a time I even sometimes wet the bed and was reduced to hysterical tears.

I now realise that my respite carer Heather White was an inspiration in my life to get things right and help others although I was rather cheeky with her and less than gratified at the time.

At the time I didn't understand or listen much to her, and sometimes would run off to avoid going to her house when she arrived to collect me. But once at Heather's house, I used to amuse myself in many different ways, including exploring the land of the sheep farmer Terry and playing with the sheepdog, Tie.

Tie was an adorable Border Collie and helped me to learn more about leadership and friendship. He really was a credit to his species and a great friend for me to hang and chill with.

Mum didn't give up on getting me riding and she asked me to try at a yard on Dartmoor where I had a much better time riding out on hacks across the beautiful moorland and cantering along the flatter ground. I developed good relationships with both the horses and humans at this trekking centre while learning more about how to ride. But, I still felt that something was missing in my relationship with the horses.

Back at mainstream school my struggles continued and things got even more complicated when one of my teachers asked me to act out how I might react to being offered a cigarette during drama. I responded to the question but she thought I was answering her back and exhibiting challenging behaviour. I shouted "No Go Away!" and this resulted in yet another detention. In the end this pathetic excuse for a mainstream school decided first not to include me in school activity weeks unless mum came with me and then to completely expel me for being different. I was relieved to get out of that pit though if I'm honest!

SPECIAL EDUCATION

My mother never stopped trying to help me get the support that I needed at school. After many battles, I was eventually placed in a special school called Chelfham School. But this was really a school meant for children who had physically challenging and violent behaviour, rather than children with Autism.

Many of the staff were more used to managing the pupils behaviour by 'holding for safety'. But one of the teaching staff, called June, was a great help to me. She taught history, which was really interesting for me, so I would often come to her class room during break times to read history books. My history interest was mainly in military history, but I was always interested in learning how people lived long ago, especially in ancient Greece or Rome.

June was also the English teacher. She soon saw that I had a great deal of anxiety and lots of problems around written work due to poor quality teaching and bad experiences from my past. She did everything she could to help me get my anxiety under control and start achieving again.

During this time, I had my first epileptic seizure the day before my birthday. I remember the smiley ambulance men saying I was fine, just as they do in the dramas. I started giggling and feeling a strange, but nice happy feeling whilst the paramedic showed me all the gear in the ambulance.

My second fit was far worse and I barely remember much except having an awful headache and lying on the school gym floor, then being half carried to June's classroom to lie there on a bean bag waiting for mum to fetch me. I was sick several times on the way home and it took me much longer to recover.

Speaking of medical conditions like epilepsy it should be known that I had severe asthma as well. Dental and doctors' appointments were a major struggle for me in these early days because when I sit still for more than a second I feel a very uncomfortable feeling that makes me feel I must wriggle and fidget. The way I now cope with medical appointments is to think of how ashamed Spirit and Oscar would be if I let them down by freaking out or not sitting properly.

I had to learn humour, imagination and sarcasm as well as learning different expressions and sayings. Yes I know the books all say we can't but I did. So there!

Mum had seen my talent with rhythm all my life, as I would often beat rhythms using anything I could find. Chelfham School knew of a drum teacher they thought would understand me well enough to teach me drumming. Mum took me to drum lessons with Ray, and I did really well. I actually became so good at drumming that I began regularly playing in small concerts.

Despite my successes and after many years of trying to understand the people around me I all but gave up on a normal life and it seemed barely anyone believed in me, or that I could ever live without full care, let alone in my own little house as I now do.

It felt to me as if despite my natural talents for rhythm and drums especially, few people were interested in looking on my future with a hint of positivity and so I continued my new obsession to become a great drummer in a famous band all but alone.

I feel that if my entire team of care social and therapy workers had worked properly with my mother and father as a real team and if there had been a proper system of funded help for talented people like me in place I could have done incredibly well in the world of rock music.

Two of my therapists were fantastic support to both me and my family, so despite my poor behaviour we made some good progress, especially once I had started going to drum lessons. The lessons were fantastic fun but hard work, and I became dedicated to learning and playing the drums.

A few months later my mother discovered a wonderful music group called 'Beats Per Minute' for disabled young people in the nearby city of Plymouth. I started going once a week to jam with other talented people.

With 'Beats Per Minute' I began performing in front of small audiences. Afterwards I found it hard to get over the amazing feeling of having people clap me for doing something that to me seemed easy. I was confused at people one minute telling me I was good, then telling me to be modest but not to put myself down about it either. It was, and still is an enigma for me to this day but I have given up on that one as no one even seems to have an answer!

By now it was time for me to leave Chelfham School and move on to their Kilworthy School. At first, this was a day placement, but I moved onto residential after a few months. Initially I enjoyed it, but I found it hard living with other children, many who had serious behavioural difficulties and were regularly attacking each other and the staff.

During my time at Kilworthy, my mother and her new partner Stuart took me to France to the site of the Normandy landings from World War II as they both knew I was fascinated by history. I loved it, but was shocked and horrified by the military cemeteries and can still remember the grave of a young German soldier of the same age as me who was attached to a combat engineering division; he probably didn't even understand the Nazi ideals he was fighting for. We travelled to some stunning French chateaux including one with a rather special and vast hot air balloon collection. France seems to have many lovely cafés too, and we had some truly wonderful food.

Back at school I was mainly a loner preferring to play video games in my room than hanging out with the boys in the common room, mostly as a defence against any more bullying. At several points my mum sent me back to Church Town Farm and I really loved it once I met my first real friend. I met a lovely pretty young lady called Hannah who I fell in love with.

Hannah was my first love and she lived in Bournemouth. She was the best one so far, she was kind and gentle and although she needed a wheelchair and lots of help we had an amazing time together. It was while we were dating that I had my first real birthday party on my 18th birthday, with a live rock 'n' roll band called Metz who I jammed with playing the drums.

Hannah and I became more obsessive over each other especially since I was still in Kilworthy, in Devon, so I had few real friends aside from her. I began feeling more and more depressed with my life and depending on her to help me cope more and more. Our long distance relationship petered out and in my desperation I lied to her to try to get her attention but all this did was hurt both of us in the end. I felt guilty that I had lied so I told her the truth. She was understandably heartbroken and this all but destroyed my relationship with her I still feel terrible about hurting her even now. Hannah has gone to University now and is extremely intelligent and a total inspiration to all the others with cerebral palsy. I hope Hannah has an amazing life she deserves it all!

Charlie with his young cat 'Shadow'

Charlie on a visit to his dad's house helping to salvage driftwood

from the river Tamar with a block and tackle

Charlie with his respite carer at a steam fair

Charlie proudly stands with his Roland drum kit

that he bought with his own money

Charlie jamming with the band 'Metz' at his 18th birthday party

During this time my mother met her long term partner, Stuart who is a jolly, smiley-faced, tall, thin, kind and gentle man. He speaks with a Canadian accent as he was raised there having a father in the Royal Canadian Air force He works as an analytical chemist. Stuart has been a wonderful help and fantastic role model for me. I hope I can be as cool and clever as him one day.

In my third year at Kilworthy School, I learned to be more independent and began going out on trips. Sometimes I took the bus into Plymouth with staff until I got used to it, then later on my own. But I was petrified every time and at first I really didn't like any of it at all.

My grandparents bought me a surprise gift in the form of a mirror sailing dingy. I named her Rattler after my favourite species of snake; the rattlesnake! My granddad and I worked to restore her to her full glory again as she was in poor condition when she was bought for me. I sailed her many times at Cotehele Key and at Siblyback Lake. We even had a launch ceremony with real Champagne sprayed on her bows although I didn't like Champagne when I tried some! Rattler slipped into the river on launch day and sailed like a dream for me despite her old age and the large busy river Tamar being full of other boats.

I went on a holiday with my dad, who took me away on the boat for a few days. We sailed from Plymouth up to Newlyn to escape a huge storm. Then we sailed on to The Isles of Scilly where I put in some fishing. I caught four mackerel, and chopped them up for baiting prawn pots. I remember the next morning in St Marys harbour hauling up the pots and finding a fish called a Rock Wrasse and several large edible crabs staring out at me!

It was wonderful, exciting and fun to see such things! We released them just before I left to go home. I took the Sky Airbus back home, while dad sailed the boat single handed on to the coast of Ireland then to the north of Scotland.

Not long after this I signed up to attempt the Ten Tors Jubilee Challenge on Dartmoor with a small group of students from Kilworthy, supported by some inspirational staff like Gill and Bruce. This proved to be a major opportunity to prove a strong point to those who slight disabled people or think of them as weaker.

The Ten Tors was a hard enough challenge to complete for the Army and some people have died in training, let alone the event itself. It was a huge thing for a bunch of kids from a special school, but I still remember that I led my team over the finish line with even the Army cheering us. We staggered in to have a hot cup of tea and hugs from our fans in the Army, Dartmoor rescue and families. We went to the formal presentation, where a smiling general presented us with our solid bronze medals and certificates to deafening applause.

My certificate read:

> "The Commander of 43 (Wessex Brigade) Certifies That
> Charlie Avent Has Successfully Completed The
> Ten Tors Jubilee Challenge 2007"

Looking back I now think Ten Tors was God's way of discovering if I was worthy to be with a classy horse like Spirit.

A few months later I left Kilworthy and started at Ruskin Mill College in Gloucestershire in September 2007.

I had been keen to go, as the college has a farm, an Iron Age forge and it looked as if it would be OK.

But Ruskin Mill is really an Art and Craft College for special needs young adults, and I struggled to fit in there very much.

One very high point of my first year at Ruskin Mill was the visit of His Royal Highness Prince Charles, the Prince Of Wales.

I was not at first going to be included but made myself known to all in the coffee shop and personally served his highness Earl Grey tea and fruit cake. He seemed intelligent, friendly and polite which was really lovely for me as I had no idea what to expect.

I had massive problems with anxiety and hated to be physically touched at first, so the college nurse arranged for me to try massage which oddly really helped me feel better. I soon lost a lot of my touch sensitivity although when I first tried massage I was anxious of how it might feel and first I had to meet the lady who gave me a massage so we could start to trust each other.

Ruskin Mill tried taking me for horse riding lessons at the local stable yard but this was a total disaster in the end. I was told to hit the pony I was riding then I yelled that I couldn't and was trying really hard to get it right with my riding, even though I see a literal picture of half a loaf of bread flying past me in my head whenever someone says "do a half pass". I started screaming and yelling at the poor instructor. She got very angry and I suddenly burst into hysterical tears and ran to the tack room where I hid feeling sure that the pony had been begging me not to hurt him. The Ruskin Mill support worker found me and took me down to college where they sat me down quietly with a cup of tea and said I had had an anxiety attack.

Although life was a challenge in the early days at Ruskin Mill little could I imagine that my anxiety and sensitivity was a gift in disguise.

I ran away from my carers there a lot, especially during the holidays. It seemed to me that the holiday care for those who had to stay on a 52 week basis was inadequate. It consisted of some time spent in holiday cottages with staff in places which I found boring, or staff making us get up early for college as normal and cleaning and tidying for when the other students returned in exchange for small amounts of pocket money.

Eventually after much pressure from mum, college changed the holiday care provision and began taking my friends and me on trips to include things we were interested in. Eventually I was taken on two really good trips, one to Catalonia for horse riding, and one riding holiday in Ireland not long before I left college.

I spent lots of time trying to persuade the staff to let me have a music based timetable because of my continuing love of drumming.

In the end my few friends and I rebelled against the way the college seemed to ignore our desire to become a band and began one anyway.

We were finally allowed to have one Saturday afternoon a week to jam together, but in my opinion they should have got behind us instead of trying to ignore our interests and strengths.

The group I was with was called 'Our Darkest Divide' and we had a really good time for a while but split up after our guitarist left college and I still miss him. His name was Andrew and I liked him a lot and after he left and my band collapsed I began to badly regress again.

Half way through my time at college they did finally agree to put music on my timetable but even then it was folk music and I really wanted to be a rock star like my heroes. I tried very hard to do as they asked and did well in music playing at college festivals earning the nick name 'Bonham', after the incredible drummer from Led Zeppelin, from some of the other students. I managed to organise a support worker called Chris to take me to see the band Bon Jovi on their Lost Highway tour at Twickenham which was an amazing day where they played all my favourite songs!

A few months later we went to see a band called "Bullet For My Valentine" at The Royal Albert Hall which was also spectacular. I felt the vibrations and sound going right through me!

Back in college the few lessons I did attend were mainly art with Patricia or music or textiles. I liked textiles as I love soft fabrics and I am extremely sensitive to feel and texture. But it was in art that I made my most significant discovery ever; it was in art that I met Oscar!

OSCAR THE HORSE WHO SAVED ME FROM SUICIDE

At this point I was feeling so fed up with life that I saw death as my only way out. I self-harmed almost every day right through my first and most of my second year at Ruskin Mill College; not at all because of the college. In fact I loved Ruskin Mill in many ways, but because I felt like I didn't belong anywhere and was consumed with rage and grief almost all of the time in those days.

I was running away regularly and on one occasion I ran away because I misunderstood what an angry support worker shouted at me.

Please Note: The following is taken from only my experience of the incident at Woolacombe Bay and I fully accept that although I believe this to be totally true, the truth may be somewhere between both of the perceptions of the parties involved. It should also be noted that Ruskin Mill have improved vastly since this incident. I'm not trying to attack or get at anyone.

My college decided to take my fellow students and I on a short holiday one summer and we were to camp at Woolacombe holiday park in Devon. I was struggling to find anything enjoyable in any of this as my anxiety was really high and I was therefore struggling with bed wetting. Originally I had been asked to sleep in a tent but one of the support workers let me sleep in a caravan with a student who I was able to get on fairly well with.

I remember the night when it all went wrong though very clearly. I went out for a meal with the other students and staff at a nice pub fairly close to the park. The evening started very nicely and we began to eat and had some good jokes and laughs. There was a lot of wine on the table and I suspect that the member of staff who I had the issue with had had a few glasses. I had a silly argument with one of the female staff although I can't remember the argument in detail and the next thing I knew I had a large aggressive man yelling and ranting in my face! I ran away into the bus but he cornered me at the back. I went into a meltdown and almost considered attacking him with a fire extinguisher in my anger and fear.

I thought he was about to attack or hit me. (He yelled that he would 'make sure I didn't sit down for a week' or something very like it). I ran and ran into a dark graveyard so I could hide and be closer to my lost friend Shadow where I sat sobbing shaking and asking him for help. I felt that since humans didn't seem to want me I wouldn't hold them back or cause them any more problems any longer and I felt like disappearing completely.

After a long search one of the staff found me but not before I had phoned my poor panicking mother in the middle of the night thinking she was close enough that she could pick me up and take me home. As my group and I were somewhere in Devon I thought Cornwall was close enough that I could just go home, (geography was never my strong point) and both of us were almost hysterically upset. The tutors made it sound like I was a walking behaviour problem and the cause of the entire incident. In the end we sorted it all out with my mum on the end of the phone miles away trying to calm everyone down, including the rather inept carers.

It was a stupid situation and I feel that carers should spend more time in training and learning new ways to cope as well as explaining and listening to those who they are supposed to be looking after instead of drinking then getting aggressive and angry with them and acting like children.

I found it hard to summon the courage to speak my feelings or my mind for many years and even now some things are still hard to think about, let alone talk about. One of the problems I had and still struggle with is expressing my feelings without exploding with rage when someone frustrates me. I'm better at working through my feelings now thanks to Dawn and the horses, but I still have my moments.

I feel that because many people treat Autism as a disease, it makes those who have it feel isolated and so they feel far worse. This I think directly contributed to my losing the will to live.

I first met Oscar when I was in my second year at Ruskin Mill College. I was struggling to make sense of my life, to find meaning or purpose in myself. I was so upset that I wanted to die because I hated myself for having Autism.

I would spend hours wandering around and lying around out in the grounds waiting for college to end. One day I was in Patricia, my art tutor's, class room, crying and hysterically upset, when she took me out to the stable block by her house to meet the horse Oscar.

Oscar is a now retired bay (dark brown) colour, cross country competition thoroughbred, who used to compete under the name Cleverly Bay. He has good breeding, as his grandsire was 'Clover Hill' the famous Irish Competition Stallion. The moment I met Oscar, who I had been told had a difficult start in life before being rescued by my heroic friends Jack and Mo, I felt my own self-pity become lost in a sea of love.

From the moment my hand touched his mane, I felt him in my heart like seeing a long lost brother and being reunited.

I felt like someone who was stuck in another country trying in vain to find someone to speak my own language and act as a translator for many years and then as if I had found someone just in the nick of time.

For me Oscar was a saviour in the body of a horse arriving to help me find the strength to build a new life where Charlie mattered and not silly therapists' ideas.

I am sure he was speaking to me in a powerful spiritual way. I feel that he was saying 'I love you, Charlie' and that he asked me for friendship and help in spreading the message that violence towards any animal or human being is never the answer and that real leaders can be assertive, but gentle too, at the same moment. In return he said he would help me to find ways to learn about his language, the language of Equus, and that he would never let me fall back into myself.

He said 'I'm always here in spirit if not in body'. I feel very tearful just writing about this as Oscar and I are now like brothers. Oscar then said to me 'Charlie, my people are without hope and many are enslaved, please learn the horses' language of Equus to help my people live free once more. Please help the humans learn that violence free horsemanship is the only real horsemanship'.

Oscar said to me, "Become who you were born to be and become a horse whisperer", and although I don't believe I can ever fully repay him I have since totally set my heart on becoming a horse whisperer!

Patricia could not believe what she was seeing and hearing when I turned to her with tears in my eyes telling her I wanted to become a horse whisperer as my meltdown was washed away to be replaced with a young but determined student of Equus. She looked at Oscar then at me and decided to ask for me to have a few more sessions of horse therapy with her and Oscar over the next few weeks.

However life did not give me horse therapy, life gave me a horse whisperer and a kick to get on with it no matter who or what got in my way! Carol the work experience tutor arranged for me to meet a lady called Dawn Oakley-Smith, who keeps a small herd of horses at her Natural Horsemanship stable yard called 'Heartshore Horses' on Minchinhampton Common in Gloucestershire.

Carol drove me up to Dawn's house to meet her. My first impression of Dawn was that she looked very wise and she made me wonder how much cool knowledge she had stored in her head.

I was quite nervous at first because she seemed to exert massive amounts of power but it soon became clear that Dawn was a kind, gentle but firm person who was more than happy to help those in need to learn how to help themselves.

She was not the kind of person to tolerate fools however and made this just as clear from the start! Not long after I met Dawn, I was introduced to some of her friends in particular a lovely but quiet lady called Marny Bolt who at that time Dawn was paying to help her with a fairly un-handled horse called Taz.

Charlie completing the Ten Tors Jubilee challenge with his team

Charlie with Oscar 'Cleverly Bay' the horse who saved him

and started him on his journey

Charlie's friends Erin, Lissa, India and Susanna having

a mad few minutes at the stables!

India riding Bear

Erin riding Ella

Susanna riding DJ

CHARLIE AVENT APPRENTICE HORSE WHISPERER

As soon as I arrived at Dawn's house with Carol, I was loudly welcomed by Hector (the friendly big black Labrador) who in those days Dawn kept as her friend and companion.

Dawn took us to Heartshore Stables' main field where her herd of horses were waiting to be fed with their morning hay. As soon as I saw them I knew that Heartshore was an amazing place where I would learn a very great deal about horses. I feel rather silly now but I asked Dawn if she had heard of my hero Monty Roberts. She replied, "Of course, I am a horse whisperer!"

I was totally amazed to hear this. It was the most incredible feeling, to realise exactly what was happening here! This was my destiny; to help Dawn as a Horse Whisperer apprentice. To help to save horses from certain death and to help horses and people understand one another!

Over the next three years Dawn introduced me to the silent but wonderful flight animals' language of Equus. Flight animals like deer, horses, moose, elk and zebra instinctively run away when anything they don't recognise approaches and their main thoughts are 'am I safe' and 'when or where is the next danger coming'.

All flight animals communicate using the body language of Equus and I was amazed and excited when it began to work for me and the horses started to follow me. I was so excited to be learning such a wonderful language that when Dawn taught me the basics of the Equus language I began using it on my peers and carers at Ruskin Mill with some surprising results!

Learning the language Equus helped me learn not only how to understand more of the human gestures of body language but also how to use Equus to communicate with flight animals and show them that I mean them no harm.

The first job she asked of me was making sure the hay was available to all of her horses and spread out evenly into lots of piles to prevent fights. Next we brushed and tacked up Jaffa, an old thoroughbred who I liked to cuddle. I rode him in the school area Dawn has in her field and we walked then trotted.

As I learned with Jaffa and later a Connemara pony called Cobweb, I began to realize Dawn's methods were far different from the traditional horsemanship I was used to.

Dawn taught me to lead horses with at least two or three feet of 'space' between them and myself so that if they spooked at something they would not crush my feet or knock me over. She also taught me to think ahead about situations that might arise and how I might safely deal with them.

Dawn took me later that year to meet legendary horseman Monty Roberts at one of his demos and I remember walking up to his signing stand feeling terrified and totally star struck. I said 'Hi' and stammered out "I'm worried about failing on your courses because of my learning difficulties, so please could you wish me good luck?" he replied by saying "Charlie, you must make your own luck and forget about your weak points" and he told me he didn't think I needed luck anyway!

Then he wrote in my book:

"To Charlie, Good Learning

And Go For It!

Monty"

I then went to see Kelly Marks and asked her about the Intelligent Horsemanship courses and how best to proceed with regard to my taking part. Kelly invited me to come on one of her five day foundation courses as a helper and see how I found it. I ended up really enjoying helping out on the course and was desperate to come back and get my certificate.

I finally persuaded my college to book me onto the five day foundation course and I feel proud even now with myself for showing those who doubted me that I can do it too. I think now looking back I may have taken what Monty said a little too literally when he told me to go for it!

I have since discovered that because many young Autistic people are like young or wild horses it can be helpful to use similar methods to aid communication. I now use rounded, soft body language and lack of eye contact when speaking too other Autistic people.

I try to keep my voice calm and quiet, trying not to sound like I'm angry or shouting around them as we are sensitive to this. Some say Autistic people are confused by body language, but I find it helps to use the language of Equus and that by learning the language of Equus Autistic people can find it easier to understand body language and gestures.

A few months later I went on a five day foundation course with 'Intelligent Horsemanship' and Kelly Marks. I found Kelly and her team to be kind, helpful and supportive so despite my initial anxiety I quickly settled into the course and had a wonderful time.

I felt proud having my photo taken holding up my certificate and feel that I can now achieve more with horses than I could ever have alone in this crazy and sometimes cruel world.

Dawn seemed impressed by my achievements on the five day foundation course but Ruskin Mill made a much bigger fuss of it. Rather than just simply saying well done, they took the certificate straight off me wanting to present it at my leaving day as part of their ceremony, but I was not impressed by this as I felt a little cheated despite their paying for my course in the first place!

MY TRAVELS TO CATALONIA FRANCE AND IRELAND

I was desperate to visit another country and had been eager to go somewhere new ever since Oscar had helped me regain the will to live. However just as I got into my 2nd year at Ruskin Mill, the yearly cultural trips were all cancelled due to lack of money due to the economic meltdown. Honestly, they say I have learning difficulties but it wasn't me who sent the world into financial meltdown!

Out of despair I asked my college if there was any chance that I might visit another country during holiday time and was told that they were planning on taking me to Catalonia in Spain to ride horses in the mountains and explore the Spanish Pyrenees.

We went in the summer holidays when many of the other Ruskin Mill students were at home. It was a very exciting, but anxious time for me travelling to another country.

At the airport I was searched because the zip in my jeans set off an alarm. This was a very difficult thing for me to know how to cope with. I was petrified and shaking all over during the security checks as touch is something I find very hard to deal with unless I am doing the touching because my Autism means I'm very sensitive to the world around me.

We arrived in Spain to amazing heat and stunning scenery, with mountains stretching far into the distance.

I found Catalonia rather overloading at first, but as the wonderful emotional adventure began to unravel, I became more relaxed and I soon began loving every second of it.

Once in Catalonia we were met by some friends and family of one of the Ruskin Mill tutors called Mark who was the leader of our trip. Many of the people in his family only spoke Catalan so he had to translate for us. We drove for several hours leaving the airport and passing by vineyards mountains and towns. At last we stopped for lunch and sat outside a small cafe drinking coke and eating. The locals all seemed very friendly and I was surprised at their ability to make themselves understood even though I was hopeless with speaking French let alone Catalan although I do echo what people say sometimes like a parrot!

My dream super power would be to be able to fluently speak read understand and write every single language in the universe! Imagine the world of new friendships and learning that you would unlock!?

We left the cafe behind and drove on to Mark's sister's castle in the mountains which is literally exactly what it is! A vast mountain-top castle with stunning views all around. I literally climbed out of the backseat of the car wondering if we were on top of the earth! Every direction I looked in seemed to be empty sky to the horizon.

We arrived at the campsite and met our horses almost right away. We had to prove that we were safe to ride them before taking them out on the mountain passes.

We stayed in a small town called Baga and went for many wonderful rides while vultures and eagles soared above us around the peaks of the mountains.

We also swam in the campsite swimming pool and relaxed while watching eagles circle overhead and weave through the peaks of the mountains as the hot sun beat down from a cloudless blue sky.

While we were riding in the mountains I decided to stand up on my horse who was called Priska and have photos taken. Our guide found this very surprising as we were far away in the middle of the forest and in known wolf country!

I saw all kinds of large and interesting insects in Catalonia and I also saw a snake on the track as we rode along but the poor thing was dead and so I dismounted and buried it respectfully. Many people find snakes scary but I find them interesting and feel sorry for them when I hear that people kill them.

I know how hurtful it feels when someone is scared of you and I know the feelings of anger this triggers.

We met a wise herbal healer in the mountains where we stopped for our lunch and we had a lovely picnic in her beautiful garden.

We also drove into France and swam in the Mediterranean Sea. When we were swimming in the sea we swam out to a raft far out in the bay. We took turns trying to dive to the bottom but it was far too deep for me and I almost had an asthma attack trying! I also swam under the water watching the colourful fish swim past and around me.

On the raft were three tanned and slender blond haired young French ladies who I rather liked but the language barrier was extremely annoying so conversation was nearly impossible let alone flirting, although I got the distinct impression that they understood more than they let on. I think they were perhaps hoping I would give up and leave!

Charlie standing tall in Catalonia

The healer's home in the mountains of Catalonia

Charlie   exploring   the   forest   pass

I fell in love with France and Spain and I was sad to return to England. When our plane touched down in Bristol airport it was cold, wet and rainy.

I was desperate for a cup of strong English tea as I had gone without tea for over a week whilst in Catalonia so my first stop was the kitchen of the Ruskin Mill house I was staying in that holiday.

In Catalonia and France they don't drink tea like the English do and although I thoroughly enjoyed the food and sweet tasting wine, I must admit tea is by far my favourite drink.

Shortly after my return from my Spain and France trip with Ruskin Mill, I was invited to accompany my father on his thirty six foot long sailing boat 'Lundy Lady' to help sail her home from La Rochelle in southern France.

My father has helped me write about our time in France as I was unable to remember all the place names and also because he is a sailing man and knows the correct terms for seamanship.

We flew out to La Rochelle and were soon aboard the boat readying her for sea. While we were in La Rochelle we explored the town and ate in one of the local cafes.

From La Rochelle we headed to Les Sables D'Olonne, the home of the Vendee Globe race fleet. Then onto the entrance of the Gulf Of Morbihan, a beautiful inland sea where we waited for the tide to go up to Le Bono at the head of the Auray river.

We went ashore and ended up clambering through the bushes until at last we finally got to a track which we then followed to a small but lovely village.

On we then sailed to L'Orient submarine base with its wreck close to the old U-boat pens. I thought at first that the wreck was a U-boat but I think now that it was a bombed-out military transport ship of some kind as many of the German U-boats were scuttled by the allies at the end of the war off the coast of Ireland.

We went exploring ashore and found a wonderful inter-Celtic Festival, with square rigged sailing ships and Irish music. We met two lovely young pretty girls who gave us a lift into the festival (I think they were keen on me because I'm the handsome one!). I was overwhelmed by the sights at the festival, especially the Viking longboats and music, not to mention food and smells and displays of all kinds. I decided that I was too overwhelmed and tired to stay and see the entire festival but I must say it was quite a sight!

On we sailed to Benodet past the Ile De Groix and into the Odet river. We went fishing with some French kids into the early hours of the morning and my father had to remind me that we needed to sleep at least for a little while!

Leaving La Rochelle harbour

L'Orient submarine base in France

Charlie rowing on the river in France

View from the land of Fort de Burthaume, near Brest in France

Charlie sailing his dad's boat Lundy Lady

In the deep marina I fished for bream although I caught nothing because I'm not so good at fish whispering!

We went to Camaret, through the notorious Raz Du Sein which is an area of extremely vicious tides where I fished with my boat rod in water over a mile deep and caught so many mackerel that we didn't know what to do with them all!

We then went ashore to visit a Napoleonic fort from the Hornblower books where we saw the old cannons being fired as part of a play. Then we returned to the boat to set the lobster pots overnight. We woke the next morning to find that we had caught crabs and a young conger eel. When my father saw the conger eel he almost jumped overboard in shock!

As my father was worried that the weather was closing in and about to get very nasty, we kept the crabs alive in a bucket all the way back across the channel to the historic English naval port of Plymouth and on the way home we saw dolphins leaping beside our boat in the moonlight and I still remember lying in my bunk half asleep when dad shouted 'Charlie! Dolphins!' I ran up on deck in time to see a large Bottlenose Dolphin brake the surface showing me its dorsal fin and head before diving once more. This sight thrilled me but also made me think of the mariners of old who told stories of mighty sea creatures!

We made crab cakes upon returning home and then we made one last boat trip to see the firework competition in Plymouth Sound.

My dad reckons the total distance we must have sailed was approximately 800 nautical miles but it felt a lot further in a thirtysix foot long boat surrounded by sea!

It was during my last year at Ruskin Mill College that I asked to visit Ireland during that last summer holiday. I was keen to visit the archaeological sites and to ride on the beaches in the surf, before drinking Irish beer in an Irish pub and eating Irish food. I guess I was so excited to be set free from the worst of my fears and anxieties that I wanted to get out there and live my life!

I remember getting up early on the first day to travel to the ferry port and missing the first ferry so we had a lovely adventure at the dock camping in the car which was absolutely hilarious!

In other times I would have struggled with this but I kept getting up and going down to the ferry terminal to look at the maps of Ireland hanging on the wall as I was unable to sleep.

We finally got onto the correct ferry at the correct time and made a night passage to Ireland where we drove off the ferry and found ourselves looking at an incredible sight... fields of horses, mainly thoroughbred and similar types I thought, stretching into the distance and many wonderful sights to watch as we sped along. We stopped for a traditional Irish breakfast which was fantastic and everything a good breakfast should be, then we drove on to our first base near Dingle in County Kerry.

The next day we visited the riding stables and were introduced to our horses. I demanded to ride an Irish sport horse and was introduced to a stunning sixteen hands high chestnut mare called Chell.

I didn't dare tell anyone the truth that I had never ridden a powerful eventer like Chell before for feared I might not get the chance to ride her!

We galloped along Dingle beach dodging the crowd of dogs, children and people then I took her into the sea and had my photo taken as she pranced and danced. Chell taught me what I could expect from Spirit and all the noble sport horses I was to meet in the future.

I love and miss Chell very much she showed me the spirit of Ireland and how fantastic the hospitality of the Irish people is.

After our wonderful beach ride we changed into our swimming things then got onto Irish cob ponies bareback to swim on them in the sea. I was very nervous with only my swimming shorts and hat on in the deep water but trusted the stunning grey pony to keep us both safe despite the choppy sea washing over us.

I was, and still am, awed by the strength, power and versatility of all horses and ponies. I can't remember the name of the cob I swam in the sea on but I do remember having the time of my life in Ireland!

The next stable yard we visited was OK but wasn't as friendly or as nice as Chell's had been. I was shown to a powerful and fiery sport horse gelding called Monty who I later learned was directly descended from the famous Irish stallion Clover Hill. Monty was amazing but frightening too and if I'm honest I was glad to leave that place alive!

The next day we visited another part of Dingle and took a boat trip where we saw the Dingle dolphin Fungi leaping beside the boat. I love dolphins and really want to swim with them one day.

Shortly after this I bought a professional Bodhran Irish drum which is fully tuneable and we all spent time trying to work out how to play it.

I had a small head start as my drum teacher had given me some pointers prior to my trip. Our last night in Ireland was spent in a 5 star luxury hotel as Ruskin Mill College had made a good, but rather expensive, mistake booking our accommodation!

On our way home we had a problem with the car. It completely broke down and left us stranded near a beautiful old churchyard with many Celtic ruins close by. While we waited for a tow truck we explored the area and I did some work on my Bronze Art Award project which earned me an equivalent to a C grade GCSE while sitting in the bright afternoon sun.

Eventually a tow truck came and a taxi arrived to so we were able to get to the ferry port with a special police escort to go home!

As soon as I got home to Gloucestershire I asked Patricia to get my photos printed out ready to go home and then arranged to visit my family in Cornwall to show them my photos of all my wonderful adventures in Ireland. I was still very excited and totally singing Ireland's praises so I was fairly fixated on my new favourite place.

My family were pleased to see me so happy and full of life so they were happy too and we had a lovely time talking all about Ireland and drinking tea!

Charlie riding Chell in the sea on Dingle Beach

in Ireland and living the dream!

Charlie just about to go swimming in the sea on an Irish Cob

Charlie at a local Irish pub jamming!

MY IDEAS AND CONCEPTS ON AUTISM

I am now going to introduce you to my methods and concepts around Autism and learning difficulties. Most of my ideas were inspired by Oscar and the other wonderful horses and people I have met including Monty Roberts.

Dawn at Heartshore Horses gave me opportunities and freedom that were unmatched anywhere before.

I believe we should do our best to make it easy for our friends and family members with Autism to behave the way that we wish them to, even if it means meeting them half way. The point is reward the 'tries' and help them learn from mistakes. Over protective care is counterproductive in the long term and only increases their dependence on others. Our target should always be to increase independence and to aid and promote greater self-worth in those who have Autism through facilitating learning regardless of disability.

If we truly wish to build a human empire of peace, scientific discovery and exploration we must harness the awesome creative power of the Autism spectrum and help those on it learn a useful role in society!

People often give me sympathy for being, as they see it, disabled. But I see my Autism as a challenge and a journey as well as a tool which is only able to be a disability if one allows it to be one.

Although I still get sensory overload in crowded or noisy rooms, I mainly manage it by thinking of horses or going into my zone which is hard to explain to neuro-typical people, although all horses know what I mean as do many Autistic people.

My zone is a kind of space in my head that helps me keep my feelings thoughts and emotions in check. Emotional control can be hard for those with Autism, especially in crowded places or in busy areas and so I find it helps to focus on the now.

At Heartshore Horses I am a volunteer helping Dawn to develop empathic and sympathetic ways to educate and aid the growth of people and animals that have had challenges in their lives.

One of our most powerful methods for helping both horses and humans to understand each other better is to teach about boundaries and personal space, as successful relationships cannot be formed without firm boundaries being established first. Boundaries lead to trust which in turn leads to successful relationships which is the basis of friendship.

When working with an autistic child my mentor and I first like the individual to be able to express themselves freely as long as they do not cross our boundaries. When working with horses we employ the same methods as we would with an autistic individual, we establish firm boundaries with the horse through Natural Horsemanship techniques, thus creating a basic level of trust between horse and human and we allow the horse to express himself freely.

We don't punish self-expression, we rather encourage it and rather than strapping the horse down, we let the horse we are working with jump around if he wants to.

If the horse chooses to jump around we ask that he does so more and that he shows us the respect that we deserve by giving us plenty of space while expressing himself in ways that will not cause damage or injury to humans or animals.

When working with the autistic children, Dawn and I have found it helpful to use positive and negative instant consequences to encourage positive good behaviour in the individuals just as my friend and mentor Monty Roberts does.

Through my experiences of education I have been able to build a plan with Dawn to help her with her new education system at Heartshore. This system is based on causing the horses and/or humans to want to learn instead of being forced into situations where they are forced to learn and fit a mould and then end up failing miserably.

We teach based on the students' abilities, interests and needs. When I was in school they tried to force me to learn lessons based on the national curriculum rather than what I was interested in or good at.

I have since discovered that by working with the strengths and interests of an individual it leads to them to try harder and achieve more. We have found that you can build other subjects into activities and in my opinion there is no such thing as special educational needs; rather more a problem of teaching difficulties.

In many cases teachers have poor quality training and far too much 'red tape' as well as poor resources to cope with while trying to teach large classes full of bored children who often feel isolated and that they have no say in their education and then feel that school is not worth their time.

One of the most important methods we have at Heartshore is the 'Horse Boy' method developed by Rupert Isaacson where Autistic children can sit or lie on a horse without the saddle to have sensory time and relax. We also often put a child on the horse and 'long line' from behind and with this approach the child is able to feel the fun and excitement of riding while we remain in control from the ground. This is particularly useful if we have adults or bigger children wanting to ride and we can give them a fun and safe way to learn.

Heartshore is a place where people learn to respect each other for who they are. We do not expect others to change their personalities to fit us instead we try to be emotionally and spiritually intelligent to everyone's individual needs personalities and wishes. We embrace new personalities and chart them through astrology, in this way we are able to help each other learn to co-exist and even to use their strengths to make up for each other's weaker points in team work.

One important lesson in the value Autism plays in our lives, is that computers and the internet were developed mainly by people on the Autistic spectrum. In fact many of history's greatest inventors and scientists were Autistic.

SPIRIT OF SUMMER'S RAIN

From the start of my time learning from Dawn, and as I became more confident, competent and able, it became apparent that more than anything I wanted to have a horse of my own. As this seemed to me to be impossible I waited as long as I could before I finally cracked and asked Dawn how expensive they really were to keep. She replied, ''We can keep them very cheaply here at Heartshore''.

After many weeks of discussions, meetings and anxious waiting for me, my mum and my Ruskin Mill house parents, the news that I was to have a horse of my very own made me cry!

And I had already decided on the name, 'Spirit'! Inspired by the animated children's movie about a wild mustang whose wild spirit no one can break.

I first met 'Spirit' on a lovely warm sunny day in May. It all happened after a phone call from a horse breeder who had seen my advertisement, knew that I was looking for a young horse, and had just the one! We arranged to visit the stables and I was introduced to a young and very handsome colt.

Although I instantly liked his spirited nature, Dawn and I decided not to buy him. We went on to the next paddock where I met a young Irish sport horse cross thoroughbred called 'Summer's Rain', whose father was the famous coloured sport horse stallion 'Masterpiece' and who now stood up on a mound in her field and pawed the ground lowering her head as if bowing me into her life before she came barging over to meet me. I knew that Summer's Rain was Spirit and that 'Spirit Of Summer's Rain' had chosen me. I gave her a big hug around her wonderful soft powerful neck and although Spirit backed up feeling a little unsure about this, I continued to hug her and whispered in her ear that I would do anything and everything I could to make her happy. The moment I met Spirit I had immediately fell in love!

The breeder wanted a quick sale and so was happy to agree on a fair price and Spirit arrived at 'Heartshore Horses' on June 20th 2010.

I remember the sunny hot day when Spirit arrived at Heartshore well. The way Spirit came shooting out of that lorry looking scared stiff and trotting all around me as well as barging all over me in her anxiety trying to work out where she was and what was happening. I won't deny feeling extremely anxious about just what on earth I had taken on when I realised how green (untrained) Spirit was! It's funny to think that within six weeks Spirit learned that I was her friend and began following me around of her own free will!

Spirit and I have a wonderful relationship. She is an extremely easy and kind horse despite still being young and I don't believe you could ask for a better teacher than a young horse, although I don't recommend taking on a young horse without expert help available.

We play and learn as partners and I have been training her almost totally unaided. I never use pain or force when training her, we use the methods of 'Silversand Natural Horsemanship' and the 'Monty Roberts Join Up' method.

Spirit and I are now on a mission together to try to help and inspire those with difficulties and their families and friends to try Natural Horsemanship and to NEVER give up on their dreams. Spirit is very well looked after and has an equine osteopath as well as one of the world's leading equine dentists, a fantastic vet and a very good hoof trimmer called Mell who from the start was there to help me teach Spirit about the farrier in a very positive way that meant no stress or rushing around for anyone.

STARTING & TRAINING SPIRIT OF SUMMER'S RAIN

We began Spirit's formal preparation for ridden work first with 'The Monty Roberts Join Up' method of letting Spirit go loose in a large round pen and moving her around it in both directions twice in each direction. Once we had Joined Up, we then put a saddle on Spirit and let her go loose again to express herself freely and buck as much as she likes.

The idea is that Spirit learns to control her anxieties and fears to an extent and can think rather than react to each situation. I want my horse to choose to be my partner just as my hero and friend Monty Roberts trains his horses. Spirit bucked strongly with the first saddle of her life and even reared a few times, but only for a few minutes, before she soon settled down to canter nicely in both directions around the round pen and then Join Up with Dawn once more.

Next we used the long lines to teach Spirit to stop and go and to turn when asked with the rein aids.

Here came the greatest moment in my life, when I was legged up onto Spirit's saddle and lay over her. Spirit was very calm and seemed not to care, so within 3 days of work to train her I ended up sitting upright on Spirits sacred back!!! We had to halt work to train Spirit for two days on one weekend as Dawn was away.

Two days later Dawn was back and she legged me up again and I lay over Spirit before I suddenly felt her shiver then she exploded into a fierce rodeo of bucking. I had to leap clear to avoid injury as Spirit fell onto her side grazing herself. She struggled to her feet and shook herself in a dignified way before casually lowering her head to graze.

Dawn and I were extremely worried in case she would now be traumatised and would need lots of special work to 'fix her' again so we could get her back on track but I got almost straight back on again with Dawn helping me and things were ended for the day on a happy very positive note.

This little blip in Spirit's training turned out to be a blessing in disguise however, as Spirit has since decided to look after both herself and her rider much more carefully and Dawn and I learned an important lesson in starting young horses without such breaks in their training.

These days I can ride Spirit wherever I like and she looks after me despite an incredibly strong will. On her 5th birthday, my friends and I took our horses on a pub ride and this was a wonderful experience for both myself and Spirit as we had to dodge the cows and horses on the common and try to keep ourselves and each other safe by all pulling together with teamwork.

I must say that keeping Spirit naturally and training her naturally has helped both of us to grow stronger both physically and mentally. It has really helped to create a good healthy relationship between the two of us and despite what some people have told me that Spirit cannot possibly live without a stable or shoes, because she is a thoroughbred ex-sport horse, she can and does.

THE POWER OF AUTISM MEETS NATURAL HORSEMANSHIP

Dawn has since begun using a method based on the 'Horse Boy Methods', and has worked alongside Rupert Isaacson, author of the bestselling book 'The Horse Boy'. I remember the day Dawn announced that Rupert was coming to do a demo at Heartshore, I was very excited to meet and work with him although when we did the main demo we struggled with the weather and Dawn and he had differing views on how horses should be trained.

Now that I have helped out with some of his demos and trainings I think Rupert Isaacson is a lovely man who has an amazing amount of knowledge on Autism and although we all have very different opinions on horsemanship we had some lovely talks about his horses when I helped him with his demo at Heartshore Horses.

Dawn and I prefer a more natural approach to horsemanship and he prefers a more traditional approach so we respect each other's opinions. Everyone has their own ideas and I'm not here to be rude or try to force anyone out of their comfort zone, I'm just obsessed with horses and horse welfare and I'm sure that all horses are gods pretending to be animals.

DEBUT DEMO

I was contacted by some friends of mine who run a lovely charity riding centre in Taunton Somerset called 'The Conquest Centre For Disabled Riders' to say they were having an open day and asking if Spirit and I would like to be a part of it with a small demo. I said I was honoured and accepted so off we went to Somerset with Spirit in a hired horse trailer and me feeling very anxious about taking her somewhere new! We arrived to find my Facebook marketing had worked overtime and that over 300 people had come to hear my talk and meet Spirit! The open day was a success and it taught me valuable lessons that I have since used in subsequent demos. Spirit and I were given a stable and no less than the head groom herself came to give Spirit her hay! Spirit and I will never forget that wonderful day surrounded by friends and family and I don't think Spirit has ever had such a warm friendly welcome before or since. On the journey home Spirit was keen to stay behind but with very gentle persuasion she loaded to go home again.

OFFICIAL COMMENDATION

I heard I had been nominated and shortlisted for a 'Leading The Learner Voice' award via email from Ruskin Mill college but I barely thought much of it until we went to the ceremony in London. Dame Ruth Silver DBE suddenly called me up to receive an official certificate of commendation for my efforts to improve education, especially for those with complex needs through public speaking. I was completely overwhelmed and dumbstruck as the room erupted with applause and had to be nudged to get up and receive my award. It was a truly remarkable moment as I rarely win or get awarded anything.

Charlie receives a certificate of commendation for his work on improving education for others with Autism

NATURALLY CLASSICAL

A few weeks passed and then I had an exciting email from a delightful lady by the name of Jenny Rolfe who has a wonderful method for working with horses using core breathing and breath energy. Jenny said she had seen my story online and wanted me to come and meet her three Iberian dressage stallions. Jenny was in the process of finding a new house but invited me to visit her yard and meet her horses. The first time I visited the weather had not been good so the stallions were less keen to show off their moves, but the second time I visited Jenny did a spectacular mini-demo for my mum and I with her horses at liberty and clearly really enjoying and taking pride in their work! Although I love Jenny's three stallions Maestu, Habil and Delfin very much I have fallen in love in particular with two of them.

Habil and Delfin are the two who I felt most connected to and feel friendship in particular with. Seeing Jenny and her inspirational work was awesome but when she got me to try working with the stallions myself and let me have my photo taken with them it was a wonderful end to a fantastic day! Her husband Barrie cooked my mum and me a lovely lunch and then Jenny presented me with a signed copy of her first book, 'Breathe Life Into Your Riding' and to this day I treasure it and the memories it stirs. I had been looking for a better way to learn dressage and understand life more from the horses' perspective and I must say Jenny is definitely onto something!

Dawn now runs therapy camps for autistic children and their families at Heartshore Horses in Gloucestershire and these are mainly based on the Horse Boy methods combined with Natural Horsemanship. We even use liberty work and trick trained horses to try to inspire the Autistic children to try having fun with horses.

During our 'Horse Boy' camps and Autism work I meet many lovely people but two Autism families really stand out as special.

The Underhill family were one such family with their two children Dylan, the Autistic animal-and-fun-loving boy, and Tehya, the pretty little girl princess who loves guinea pigs and rabbits, mum Natasha and dad Tom. Tom reminds me of a trendy sporty schoolboy with his grin and warm cheerful persona. Natasha is a tough but fair Autism mum and both Tom and Tash are very kind thoughtful people who are always ready for a laugh. Working with the Underhill family has taught me a great deal about Autism and how families work.

The family often comes down from London to ride at Heartshore and play. One of the best activities is watching my friend India (Dawn's daughter) riding at speed with young Dylan in front of her on a horse while he shouts Ready Steady Go! And giggles almost endlessly! This is a child who doctors would say has Autistic Spectrum Disorder but he has proved that there is nothing wrong with him, only that he was made a different way for a different role in life.

The other Autism family that stands out for me is Scot's family. Scot is at the moment not yet speaking verbally and is often aggressive and violent when he can't do something he wants to do or feels unwell but I think there is far more intelligence there than he is ever given credit for.

The boy is a natural born artist with a wonderful talent for making sculptures in moving water, by flicking it up to make geometric shapes that can be captured for the enjoyment of less able beings by high speed cameras. Scot is also learning to ride on the horses and is progressing well in this area. Scot's mum and dad are lovely too and their dog Dotty always seems happy to see me-especially if I'm eating!

At Heartshore Horses, as I have already stated, we use Natural Horsemanship methods, keeping all our horses as naturally as possible, which seems to be a far more effective as therapy not just for Autistic clients but also on those with mental health issues or people who are just having a hard time generally in life.

Horses kept and trained naturally are happier and less tense, therefore they are able to give more to clients and help them learn.

I really enjoy the 'Horse Boy' camps as we always have interesting new people come and I enjoy chatting and getting to know new friends as you can probably tell from this book!

I do volunteer work as an assistant on these camps and do my best to look after those who need special help as well as giving parents and carers my somewhat strong, but totally valid, opinions and advice on Autism.

On one such camp I met a lovely lady called Heidi who invited me to come back to Wales and help out with a stunning but anxious young horse called Star. Star was a Welsh cob with a strong will and a stronger personality but she was also stunning to look at having been semi-wild on the mountain slopes for many years.

I fell in love with Star instantly although it took several hours for me to start to get her trust. My friend India has since taken on and trained Star up as a riding horse. India has done a fantastic job of helping her become braver! Heidi's Welsh hospitality and fantastic cooking really made my Welsh adventure; especially the amazing cooked breakfasts!

Spirit and I are working on learning as many liberty based games as we can so that as my demos progress each time with Spirit, people can see our bond and be inspired to share ideas and experiment with more Natural Horsemanship methods.

In the liberty games I will let Spirit make the choice to stay with me without a rope and if she moves away from me I take control of her direction asking her to move around and teach her using my gestures and body language that I would prefer that she stays with me and tries to listen, but no one has the right to say "You must or I will hurt you" to any human or animal.

I enjoy telling the visiting families about my life changing experience with Oscar and enjoy introducing Spirit to all those who wish to meet to her.

Spirit and I are now setting out to try to inspire others to try Natural Horsemanship through giving talks and telling my story.

My longer term plans with Spirit are to help train Riding for the Disabled Association staff and horses in Autism-friendly methods using Monty Roberts methods and to acquire my 'Monty Roberts Instructors Certificate' but of course money is very limited.

Spirit and I want to inspire others with disabilities or difficulties to just carry on regardless and focus on their strengths and interests and even to try voluntary work.

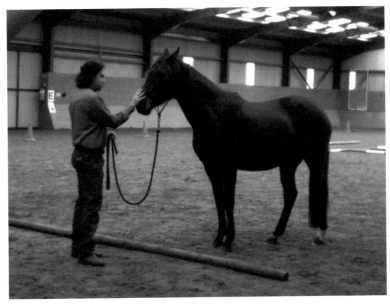

Charlie and Spirit doing a demo at the Conquest Centre open day

Playing with Spirit and an umbrella

Charlie and Spirit at Liberty during a

photo shoot for Horse Magazine

Charlie playing with Spirit over jumps at Liberty

Charlie and Delfin the wise kind Stallion owned by Jenny Rolfe

Spirit and Charlie demonstrate at The Complete Horse and Rider

Extravaganza in Cheltenham

BUMPS IN THE ROAD

By this time I had made my story fairly well known on Facebook and other social media as well as several large equestrian magazines, but with this new found freedom to share my story came a great many new challenges.

My Facebook profile became the repeated target of fake profiles and cyber bullies not to mention online stalking. I even had my profile hacked on several occasions too and some silly and mostly rude messages sent to some of my friends. I remember once getting an angry phone call from my friend asking me why her clients were getting rude and odd messages from my profile and I totally panicked and rushed home to change all my settings and passwords! It got so bad at one stage that I considered leaving Facebook altogether and finding a new way to tell my story but then I realised that letting them beat me would disgrace Oscar and all he had done for me. A particularly hard one was an online stalker and troll who first appeared friendly and even claimed to have the exact same story as me. I made the mistake of befriending them, I thought this might be interesting and might be fun to have a new friend but then the troll's true self surfaced and they began spreading lies and telling everyone on my friend list that I was a bully in an attempt to turn everyone against me. Thank goodness I was able to show evidence of the vile disgusting messages they and their friends were sending me to the police and report them to Facebook. To this day I will never understand why I was targeted by these sad people but I guess most were jealous of my new life and perhaps even threatened by my strong beliefs and opinions on Autism.

These photos were taken on the wonderful day Charlie and Spirit

first met each other and chose to become partners

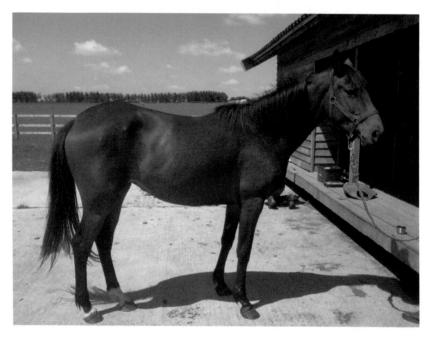

Spirit's first day at Heartshore

Charlie riding Spirit without tack!

Spirit having fun and choosing to stay standing on Tarp!

Charlie and Spirit pose during a photo shoot for Horse Magazine

THE APPRENTICE MEETS THE MASTER

In November 2012, we had a phone call not long before Monty Roberts was due to do a demo near Gloucester at Hartpury College for his Jubilee tour, to say that he had heard all about my story and wanted me to come and be part of his demonstration.

Let me tell you that to speak about my Autism and do a Join-Up in front of everyone with Kelly Marks's eighteen hands high hunting horse Harry was no easy task, and I considered it a great honour especially as Horse and Country TV also asked to interview me! As you can imagine I was honoured but nervous as I walked into Hartpury College main arena to meet with master horseman and horse whisperer Monty Roberts before the demo and plan how things would go.

Monty and I sat on chairs with my friend Dawn and had a cup of tea and a wonderful talk first about my experiences then about some of his and then he told me about his life in Western competitions as well as telling me that wild Mustang horses are "very intelligent and kind and a pleasure to work with" in answer to my questions. Monty then showed me a beautiful clasp knife engraved with his name and the date that he won it as a prize.

Dawn and I then settled down to watch Monty's team choosing the horses for the demo. Some people are sceptical of Monty and some claim he trains horses beforehand but I can tell you categorically that the horses are never trained before his demos because I was there watching the team and keeping an eye! The demo began later that evening with Monty and Kelly helping people understand their horses. Then half way through his demo Monty asked me to do my part.

I was terrified to speak but this feeling soon subsided when Monty Roberts was with me speaking to the crowd and introducing me. Suddenly I felt a strong feeling of passion and determination wash over me and began to walk up and down in front of over 1000 people telling my story. When I spoke that day I was speaking from controlled anger about the way I had been treated in the past and a determination to make a better tomorrow for others with additional needs at any cost! If only I had known what wonderful people I would meet and the fantastic adventures I would have thanks to that one demo with Monty Roberts and Kelly Marks! Monty spoke about his time working with combat stress in soldiers with Post Traumatic Stress Injuries and the fantastic success he has had. When I was with Harry doing Join Up, nothing existed anymore except him and me. Although my Join-Up movements were ok, I struggled a little to draw Harry in toward me although he did Join-Up with me in the centre. My demo with Harry sparked a wonderful applause but Harry was at first unsure about this and had to have a hug from both me Monty and Kelly. Monty took the rope from me and hugged me grinning widely while the anxiety drained away from me. He then told the entire audience that he was making me his newest team member and invited me to come to his Flag Is Up Farms ranch in California America to help him with working with combat veterans with PTSI (Post Traumatic Stress Injury) and he also promised to take my letter to Her Majesty the Queen of England and put it right into her hand for me next time he visited her!

Charlie with Monty Roberts and Kelly Marks during the demo

Spirit and Charlie often make tunnels of Tarp to
test and improve their relationship

Spirit and Charlie are learning both Bitted and Bitless Dressage together so they can perform freestyle Dressage to music

Charlie, Spirit and Dawn

Not long after my demo with Monty Roberts I had a phone call from Kelly Marks who passed me over to Monty. Monty thanked me for my help and speech at his demonstration and said he was just leaving to go to Germany on tour but he would see me soon.

A few weeks passed then as I was helping my friends hay the horses I had a phone call from Kelly Marks to say Monty was there and wanted to speak to me again, Monty told me over the phone that my letter had greatly impressed Her Majesty Queen Elizabeth II and that she was interested in my adventures with horses, so naturally I was very excited to hear this! I hope to continue helping Monty Roberts and my dream is to meet Her Majesty Queen Elizabeth II one day.

A few weeks passed then my friends and I watched me on 'Backstage Pass' with Monty Roberts and 'Top Marks' with Kelly Marks on Horse And Country TV, with Monty Roberts and Kelly Marks speaking about my Autism and doing Join-Up with Kelly's eighteen hands high hunting horse Harry! We turned it all into a party with tea and chocolate cake! I love the part where Monty asked me to give back the microphone so he could continue his demo!

I have recently attended more courses with Intelligent Horsemanship including 'Handling The Untouched Horse' near Whitney in Oxfordshire. This was a fascinating educational two days, meeting and learning how to safely handle young and totally untouched horses.

After an initial talk and theory session we were straight to practical hands on learning. My tutor Jim was fantastic and spent plenty of time explaining to me all of the methods, then demonstrating to me the ones I was still unsure about. I had a halter on a feral horse in less than 30 minutes and I still can hardly believe it!

I named the first feral horse I worked with 'Fidget' because he was sweet but wanted to move his feet lots! I was told that Fidget was a colt so I am calling him a boy although he has such long fluffy hair covering every inch of his face body and legs it was hard to tell.

The next course I attended was all about loading and leading horses that were a challenge to handle or take anywhere in a horse trailer. This was fascinating and has really helped my understanding of how to lead and load horses and ponies gently and safely.

JESSIE

Only a week or two after my adventures with Monty Roberts I was contacted by a lovely lady called Jo who owned one of the horses Monty had worked with in the demo as a tricky horse box loader. Jo told me she wanted to introduce me to her rescue ponies and told me about her work for a not-for-profit organisation called Equine Rescue Rehoming. We arranged to meet and visit the yard a few weeks later where I was very impressed with her dedication and passion for all horses and ponies. One pony on this yard really stood out for me, her name was Jessie a small bay pony with a very big personality!

Jessie had come from Ireland and although I don't know her full story I know that like many other ponies and horses she got a far from ideal start in life. She was very nervous of human contact and it was hard to get close to her in the field. Jo and I worked carefully to get Jessie more confident with people and we seem to have helped her because she has since moved on to pastures new and might soon even be rehomed!

Meanwhile I live mainly independently in a flat that I rent in Nailsworth, Gloucestershire with many friends who I regularly visit in the local community. Many of my friends are teenage girls from Heartshore who also love horses and many of them have made a very special effort to let me be part of their movie nights and social lives when appropriate, especially Erin and Lissa who are always letting me come to visit and chat with them drinking tea and sharing the latest news. I love how patient, kind and thoughtful they and their families are with my little habits and ways too.

I have many more plans for the future especially helping others with their horses and training others to be more Autism friendly through more public speaking. I hope to found a not-for-profit organisation to this end.

Jessie being brave with Tarp!

Tea break with Jessie

Charlie and Jessie out for a walk

Charlie long lines Jessie the rescue Pony

Charlie and Dufus the pony who Monty Roberts trained to load

TRAGEDY AND HOPE

I rang Oscar's former owner Mo not long after my loading course and herd the terrible news that Oscar had been injured and put down after shattering his leg while eventing.

I remember holding the phone and listening to her telling me then giving her some words of thanks and comfort before ringing off and almost dropping the phone in shock and grief. I was heartbroken and didn't know what to do with myself so I walked up to Erin's house and told her the terrible news. I then returned home and made myself a huge fried greasy breakfast as comfort food which helped me feel a little better though very full. I stayed up late on Facebook posting our story and the news that my saviour was now dead in body but inside me in spirit all over the place. I then vowed to continue my fight for horses and Autism. In Oscar's honour I will be a master horseman even though the academic side of my equine behavioural training might prove slightly harder for me than for some of the other Intelligent Horsemanship students.

REST IN PEACE OSCAR MY OLD FRIEND...

Spirit and I will continue fighting for people with additional needs everywhere and we hope to make the world a better place for all especially in areas like education and horse training and the therapy methods used with people too. I want to share how horses and learning Natural Horsemanship saved me, and I want to display our wonderful friendship via demos, which are primarily based at Heartshore Horses. But with support from Nadine at registered charity The Autism Directory, Spirit and I are now moving out to our friends' riding centres too around the UK as well as at local country shows.

We will not give up or back down in our struggle for a better more respectful world for people with different abilities or additional needs.

We both dream of an education system for England where instead of the one way street of the National Curriculum, a learner's interests and strengths are embraced in a more flexible system aimed at helping people to want to learn and succeed through Intrinsic and Incremental learning, even in areas in which they have struggled in the past.

Thanks to the registered charity The Autism Directory it really does look like I can fulfil my dream to take Spirit to visit schools and care homes giving others with additional needs a nice experience that may well inspire them to find ways around their difficulties. I met Nadine and her team from The Autism Directory as a direct result of my demo with Monty Roberts as they contacted me through Facebook telling me how much their trustee Joanne had enjoyed seeing me.

This has greatly aided my cause because not only do The Autism Directory have extensive knowledge and contacts but they are now also running a support scheme enabling autistic people who alone might struggle to have their own organisation to set up and run their own companies and organisations.

My organisation is strictly not for profit for the moment but I plan one day soon to make a living as a professional horseman, and thanks to my new friends in Wales I had a wonderful weekend running a small basic horsemanship clinic called 'Bond With Your Horse'. The event took place at the yard of event rider Amy Jane Thompson, helping the livery yard owners with spook busting and leading.

Three horses who caught my eye there aside from Amy's eventers were: a Warmblood mare called Elie who was seventeen hands high and looked magnificent but was having trouble understanding traditional single line lunging with her human Amber; a lovely Welsh cob called Lady who was having difficulties with understanding that she was not supposed to take her lovely young human Hannah for walks; and a stunning Haflinger called Brandy who seemed to have decided he was firmly in command of his human friends, had little idea about peoples personal space and was quite spooky as well as tricky to lead!

The weekend progressed well and by the end I felt I had achieved a fairly good level of bonding and trust with each horse and so had the owners.

While I was in Wales I was staying with a lady called Joanne who owns a thoroughbred horse called Apollo and keeps him on Amy Jane Thompson's livery yard. Apollo, as his name suggests, is large and magnificent but he is less than keen on travelling since an accident, so my next challenge might be helping him with this in the future.

After my Bond With Your Horse weekend had formally finished, Joanne took me out for a ride around the lanes on her friend's horse Dylan while she rode Apollo and we had a lovely wander around the block.

As I returned home I felt a strong sense of satisfaction knowing I had helped others and their horses and I felt optimistic about my own future with Spirit too.

Not long after my first proper test of my horsemanship skills with a group of live clients I decided it was time to get some help and advice of my own with Spirit. The company I chose, Simple Systems Ltd, were wonderful and their customer service was fantastic! They sent out a lovely lady called Abi who suggested a more wholesome and healthy feed plan to help Spirit get on better in winter and ever since Spirit has been calmer and more relaxed. I totally recommend Simple Systems to anyone who truly cares what they feed to their horse as Simple Systems feeds are free from additives!

Although we are dedicated to helping others, Spirit and I are severely limited in our ability to help others due to having to go through the expense and hassle of hiring horse trailers for any visits to care homes or demos at shows or public events. The Autism Directory are in the process of raising funds for a horse trailer for Spirit and I to use at the moment. We hope to do talks and demos in many new places but first we need a horse trailer and so for now most of my demos either mean borrowing horses or doing them at home.

Our message is:

Your Interests Are Your Strengths.

Charlie snuggled in the hay with Spirit

Lissa and her pony Bella out for a ride

Charlie with racing legend Kauto Star at the Lambourn open day

Kelly Marks, Charlie, American Pie and Monty Roberts

Charlie on Clyde (above) and on Sandy (below), the noble, kind and intelligent Spanish Mustangs who proved to Charlie what Monty Roberts had told him about Mustangs being truly wonderful

Charlie and Apollo in Wales

AUTHOR'S NOTE

I wrote this book to tell the true story of how a once struggling horse called Oscar rose from the ashes and saved me from suicide, but this is now bigger than that. Oscar helped me to learn how to be a part of the human race despite my teaching and educational difficulties, even after he himself had had a hard time as a foal. Anyone can become a horse whisperer if they learn to listen to the horse and commit to learning. This book is the first time I have ever properly spoken all my feelings and thoughts on Autism and horses on paper and I really hope you enjoy reading it as much as I enjoyed writing it.

My only regret is that I was unable to learn Natural Horsemanship at a much younger age.

USEFUL CONTACTS:

Autism Meets Natural Horsemanship

Read Charlie's blogs and follow his progress as he continues his work raising autism awareness and giving inspiration to others.

Charlie's website provides details of his demos and events, how you can support him and how he is getting on in the pursuit of all his passions and interests.

Plus you can continue to read Charlie's Story as it unfolds after the launch of this book.

www.autismmeetsnaturalhorsemanship.com

charlie@autismmeetsnaturalhorsemanship

Heartshore Horses

Centre for Natural Horsemanship, Riding, Education, work with Autistic Children, Horseboy and Equine Therapy.

Heartshore is a riding school, but adds something new to the traditional riding school experience. Its founding principles are to create a place to facilitate the learning and development of both people and horses, and to foster healthy relationships between the two.

Crackstone Barns, Crackstone,
Minchinhampton, Gloucestershire, GL6 9BD

www.heartshore-horses.com
dawn@heartshore-horses.com

Monty Roberts

Monty Roberts, known as the "Man Who Listens to Horses" has led an extraordinary life. An award-winning trainer of championship horses, best-selling author, Hollywood stunt man, foster dad to 47 children (in addition to three of his own) and creator of the world-renowned and revolutionary equine training technique called Join~Up.

www.montyroberts.com
askmonty@montyroberts.com

Intelligent Horsemanship

Kelly Marks founded Intelligent Horsemanship so that horse owners could get practical help at exceptional value. With her mentor, Monty Roberts, Kelly promotes respect and understanding of horses through courses, demonstrations and educational materials such as the revolutionary Monty Roberts Dually Halter.

www.intelligenthorsemanship.co.uk
info@ihhq.net

Barehoof Performance

Why barehoof trimming? In essence the hoof trim is a non- invasive procedure and the principle behind it is to remove only what is necessary to bring each foot into balance and keep the hoof disease free. Taking care of this will enable the hoof to reach optimum performance which gives obvious benefit as well as improving the general well-being of the horse.

www.barehoofperformance.co.uk
melanie@barehoofperformance.co.uk

Simple Systems

Simple System Ltd is a horse feed company dedicated to bringing you the very best forage feed diet for your horses. They pride themselves on dealing directly with customers to advise not only on good feeding practices but also responsible management, taking a full holistic approach to feeding and horse care.

www.simplesystemhorsefeeds.co.uk
info@simplesystem.co.uk

The Autism Directory

Helping Autism Families Get The Help They Need.

An online directory website that pulls together the help and support that is out there and signposts individuals with autism and their families to the help they need. The directory is populated by anyone who can share information for the benefit of others who live and work with autism in the areas of Health, Education, Treatments & Therapies, Personal Support, Living Support, Money & Legal, Recreation & Holidays, Books & Magazines and Autism Friendly Businesses (such as hairdressers).

The Autism Directory also supports individuals with Autism to live their life through their own passions and interests. Like Charlie, children and adults with Autism have a story to tell and they can help get them told.

www.theautismdirectory.com
hello@theautismdirectory.com

The Autism Expo

The Autism Expo is a specialist event in Cardiff, created to provide advice and support for parents, carers, healthcare professionals and those on the spectrum, so they can access the latest products, services and information on Autism.

www.theautismexpo.com
enquiries@thesocialhealthcareexpo.co.uk

Charlie at The Expo in Cardiff